ACHIEVE YOUR DREAMS

GOAL PLANNING
Workbook

Step by Step Method for Success

Belongs To:

_____

_____

_____

Contents

My Goal

WHAT IS MY GOAL?

Start a online "hair scrunchie business" & produce the product myself.

WHY DO I WANT TO ACHIEVE THIS GOAL?

To earn extra income while using my creativity and love for sewing.

HOW WILL I ACHIEVE THIS GOAL?

- Research similar businesses
- Find best & most efficient way to produce product
- Source materials needed for production
- Create business name & necessary tax file numbers
- Create website & social media sites for business

WHAT TOOLS WILL I USE TO ACCOMPLISH THIS GOAL?

- Sewing machine & materials
- Packaging for product
- Website
- Instagram & facebook business pages

Strategies

MY GOAL is...

Start a online "hair scrunchie business" & produce
the product myself.

STRATEGY #1

Research

Education

Source Materials

Practise

ACTION STEPS

#1 Check out competitors

#2 Find out what sells best

#3 Learn sewing skills

#4 Purchase materials

#5 Get a good production flow

STRATEGY #2

Business essentials

Business name

Research online platforms

Design logo & cards etc

ACTION STEPS

#1 Brainstorm Business name

#2 Register Business

#3 Make bank account

#4 Make online payment accounts

#5 Purchase cards & packaging

STRATEGY #3

Website

Marketing

Postage

Accounting system

Tax details

ACTION STEPS

#1 Create a website

#2 Social media setup

#3 Advertising on social media

#4 Join social media groups

#5

🎯	**MY GOALS**

Research

⊕	**TODAYS GOALS TO FOCUS ON**

Competitors

What is popular & sells the best

(if you have more than one top goal to achieve in 100 days feel free to list task for that goal also)

📶	**TO ACHIEVE MY GOAL I WILL ACCOMPLISH THESE TASKS TODAY**

Social media search of competitors ☐   ☐

Competitors names & products ☐   ☐

Lists designs & materials I like ☐   ☐

☐   ☐

☐   ☐

☐   ☐

☐   ☐

☐   ☐

☐   ☐

☐   ☐

NOTES

Reflection

AM I ACCOMPLISHING MY GOALS

YES   NO

WHAT HAVE I LEARNT IN THE PAST 25 DAYS?

It is a very competitive area so I will need to be unique and set a good and affordable price range

WHAT NEW IDEAS DO I HAVE?

I'm going to target particular niche markets, such as, pets, animals, mythical animals, as well as plain color designs.

WHAT NEW SKILLS HAVE I ACQUIRED?

Sewing to a good rhythm

WHAT CHALLENGES I HAD TO OVERCOME?

Sourcing some materials & choosing a business name

WHAT ARE MY NEXT STEPS?

Tell friends & family & get their input

"Dream big

set goals

take action."

Goals

My Goal

WHAT IS MY GOAL?

WHY DO I WANT TO ACHIEVE THIS GOAL?

HOW WILL I ACHIEVE THIS GOAL?

WHAT TOOLS WILL I USE TO ACCOMPLISH THIS GOAL?

Strategies

MY GOAL is...

_____

_____

STRATEGY #1

_____
_____
_____
_____
_____
_____

ACTION STEPS

#1 _____

#2 _____

#3 _____

#4 _____

#5 _____

STRATEGY #2

_____
_____
_____
_____
_____
_____

ACTION STEPS

#1 _____

#2 _____

#3 _____

#4 _____

#5 _____

STRATEGY #3

_____
_____
_____
_____
_____
_____

ACTION STEPS

#1 _____

#2 _____

#3 _____

#4 _____

#5 _____

My Goal

WHAT IS MY GOAL?

WHY DO I WANT TO ACHIEVE THIS GOAL?

HOW WILL I ACHIEVE THIS GOAL?

WHAT TOOLS WILL I USE TO ACCOMPLISH THIS GOAL?

Strategies

MY GOAL is...

_____

_____

STRATEGY #1

_____
_____
_____
_____
_____

ACTION STEPS

#1 _____

#2 _____

#3 _____

#4 _____

#5 _____

STRATEGY #2

_____
_____
_____
_____
_____

ACTION STEPS

#1 _____

#2 _____

#3 _____

#4 _____

#5 _____

STRATEGY #3

_____
_____
_____
_____
_____

ACTION STEPS

#1 _____

#2 _____

#3 _____

#4 _____

#5 _____

My Goal

WHAT IS MY GOAL?

WHY DO I WANT TO ACHIEVE THIS GOAL?

HOW WILL I ACHIEVE THIS GOAL?

WHAT TOOLS WILL I USE TO ACCOMPLISH THIS GOAL?

Strategies

MY GOAL is...

_____

_____

STRATEGY #1

_____
_____
_____
_____
_____
_____

ACTION STEPS

#1 _____

#2 _____

#3 _____

#4 _____

#5 _____

STRATEGY #2

_____
_____
_____
_____
_____
_____

ACTION STEPS

#1 _____

#2 _____

#3 _____

#4 _____

#5 _____

STRATEGY #3

_____
_____
_____
_____
_____
_____

ACTION STEPS

#1 _____

#2 _____

#3 _____

#4 _____

#5 _____

"When you set a goal,

your brain opens up

a task list."

Mel Robbins

100 Daily Pages

🎯 MY GOALS

TODAYS GOALS TO FOCUS ON

**TO ACHIEVE MY GOAL I WILL
ACCOMPLISH THESE TASKS TODAY**

- [ ]
- [ ]
- [ ]
- [ ]
- [ ]
- [ ]
- [ ]
- [ ]
- [ ]
- [ ]

- [ ]
- [ ]
- [ ]
- [ ]
- [ ]
- [ ]
- [ ]
- [ ]
- [ ]
- [ ]

NOTES

Day 2

🎯	MY GOALS

⊕	TODAYS GOALS TO FOCUS ON

	TO ACHIEVE MY GOAL I WILL ACCOMPLISH THESE TASKS TODAY

- ☐
- ☐
- ☐
- ☐
- ☐
- ☐
- ☐
- ☐
- ☐
- ☐

- ☐
- ☐
- ☐
- ☐
- ☐
- ☐
- ☐
- ☐
- ☐
- ☐

NOTES

🎯 MY GOALS

⊕ TODAYS GOALS TO FOCUS ON

TO ACHIEVE MY GOAL I WILL ACCOMPLISH THESE TASKS TODAY

- [ ]
- [ ]
- [ ]
- [ ]
- [ ]
- [ ]
- [ ]
- [ ]
- [ ]
- [ ]

- [ ]
- [ ]
- [ ]
- [ ]
- [ ]
- [ ]
- [ ]
- [ ]
- [ ]
- [ ]

NOTES

Date: **Day 4**

🎯	MY GOALS

⊕	TODAYS GOALS TO FOCUS ON

📶	TO ACHIEVE MY GOAL I WILL ACCOMPLISH THESE TASKS TODAY

- [ ]
- [ ]
- [ ]
- [ ]
- [ ]
- [ ]
- [ ]
- [ ]
- [ ]
- [ ]

NOTES

🎯 MY GOALS

⊙ TODAYS GOALS TO FOCUS ON

🏁 TO ACHIEVE MY GOAL I WILL ACCOMPLISH THESE TASKS TODAY

- ☐
- ☐
- ☐
- ☐
- ☐
- ☐
- ☐
- ☐
- ☐
- ☐

- ☐
- ☐
- ☐
- ☐
- ☐
- ☐
- ☐
- ☐
- ☐
- ☐

NOTES

Date: **Day 6**

MY GOALS

_____

TODAYS GOALS TO FOCUS ON

_____
_____
_____

TO ACHIEVE MY GOAL I WILL
ACCOMPLISH THESE TASKS TODAY

☐		☐	
☐		☐	
☐		☐	
☐		☐	
☐		☐	
☐		☐	
☐		☐	
☐		☐	
☐		☐	
☐		☐	

NOTES

MY GOALS

TODAYS GOALS TO FOCUS ON

TO ACHIEVE MY GOAL I WILL ACCOMPLISH THESE TASKS TODAY

- [ ]
- [ ]
- [ ]
- [ ]
- [ ]
- [ ]
- [ ]
- [ ]
- [ ]
- [ ]

- [ ]
- [ ]
- [ ]
- [ ]
- [ ]
- [ ]
- [ ]
- [ ]
- [ ]

NOTES

Date: **Day 8**

🎯 **MY GOALS**

⊙ **TODAYS GOALS TO FOCUS ON**

**TO ACHIEVE MY GOAL I WILL
ACCOMPLISH THESE TASKS TODAY**

☐ ☐
☐ ☐
☐ ☐
☐ ☐
☐ ☐
☐ ☐
☐ ☐
☐ ☐
☐ ☐
☐ ☐

NOTES

🎯 MY GOALS

⊕ TODAYS GOALS TO FOCUS ON

🪜 TO ACHIEVE MY GOAL I WILL ACCOMPLISH THESE TASKS TODAY

- ☐
- ☐
- ☐
- ☐
- ☐
- ☐
- ☐
- ☐
- ☐
- ☐

- ☐
- ☐
- ☐
- ☐
- ☐
- ☐
- ☐
- ☐
- ☐
- ☐

NOTES

Date: _____   # Day 10

⊕ **TODAYS GOALS TO FOCUS ON**

🏁 **TO ACHIEVE MY GOAL I WILL
ACCOMPLISH THESE TASKS TODAY**

	☐		☐
	☐		☐
	☐		☐
	☐		☐
	☐		☐
	☐		☐
	☐		☐
	☐		☐
	☐		☐
	☐		☐

NOTES

Day 11

🎯	MY GOALS

⊕	TODAYS GOALS TO FOCUS ON

🏁	TO ACHIEVE MY GOAL I WILL ACCOMPLISH THESE TASKS TODAY

- [ ]
- [ ]
- [ ]
- [ ]
- [ ]
- [ ]
- [ ]
- [ ]
- [ ]
- [ ]

- [ ]
- [ ]
- [ ]
- [ ]
- [ ]
- [ ]
- [ ]
- [ ]
- [ ]
- [ ]

NOTES

Date: _____   # Day 12

🎯 MY GOALS

_____

⊕ TODAYS GOALS TO FOCUS ON

_____
_____
_____

📊 TO ACHIEVE MY GOAL I WILL
ACCOMPLISH THESE TASKS TODAY

	☐		☐
	☐		☐
	☐		☐
	☐		☐
	☐		☐
	☐		☐
	☐		☐
	☐		☐
	☐		☐
	☐		☐

NOTES

Date: _____   # Day 13

🎯	MY GOALS

_____

⊕	TODAYS GOALS TO FOCUS ON

_____
_____
_____

🏁	TO ACHIEVE MY GOAL I WILL ACCOMPLISH THESE TASKS TODAY

_____ ☐   _____ ☐
_____ ☐   _____ ☐
_____ ☐   _____ ☐
_____ ☐   _____ ☐
_____ ☐   _____ ☐
_____ ☐   _____ ☐
_____ ☐   _____ ☐
_____ ☐   _____ ☐
_____ ☐   _____ ☐
_____ ☐   _____ ☐

NOTES

🎯 MY GOALS

⊕ TODAYS GOALS TO FOCUS ON

🏁 TO ACHIEVE MY GOAL I WILL ACCOMPLISH THESE TASKS TODAY

- [ ]
- [ ]
- [ ]
- [ ]
- [ ]
- [ ]
- [ ]
- [ ]
- [ ]
- [ ]

- [ ]
- [ ]
- [ ]
- [ ]
- [ ]
- [ ]
- [ ]
- [ ]
- [ ]
- [ ]

NOTES

Date: _____ # Day 15

🎯 MY GOALS

_____

⊕ TODAYS GOALS TO FOCUS ON

_____
_____
_____

📶 TO ACHIEVE MY GOAL I WILL ACCOMPLISH THESE TASKS TODAY

_____ ☐   _____ ☐
_____ ☐   _____ ☐
_____ ☐   _____ ☐
_____ ☐   _____ ☐
_____ ☐   _____ ☐
_____ ☐   _____ ☐
_____ ☐   _____ ☐
_____ ☐   _____ ☐
_____ ☐   _____ ☐
_____ ☐   _____ ☐

NOTES

Date: _____   # Day 16

MY GOALS

_____

TODAYS GOALS TO FOCUS ON

_____
_____
_____

TO ACHIEVE MY GOAL I WILL ACCOMPLISH THESE TASKS TODAY

- ☐ _____   ☐ _____
- ☐ _____   ☐ _____
- ☐ _____   ☐ _____
- ☐ _____   ☐ _____
- ☐ _____   ☐ _____
- ☐ _____   ☐ _____
- ☐ _____   ☐ _____
- ☐ _____   ☐ _____
- ☐ _____   ☐ _____
- ☐ _____   ☐ _____

NOTES

🎯 MY GOALS

⊕ TODAYS GOALS TO FOCUS ON

📶 TO ACHIEVE MY GOAL I WILL ACCOMPLISH THESE TASKS TODAY

- ☐
- ☐
- ☐
- ☐
- ☐
- ☐
- ☐
- ☐
- ☐
- ☐

- ☐
- ☐
- ☐
- ☐
- ☐
- ☐
- ☐
- ☐
- ☐
- ☐

NOTES

🎯 MY GOALS

⊕ TODAYS GOALS TO FOCUS ON

TO ACHIEVE MY GOAL I WILL ACCOMPLISH THESE TASKS TODAY

	☐		☐
	☐		☐
	☐		☐
	☐		☐
	☐		☐
	☐		☐
	☐		☐
	☐		☐
	☐		☐
	☐		☐

NOTES

Date: _____

Day 19

🎯 **MY GOALS**

⊙ **TODAYS GOALS TO FOCUS ON**

📶 **TO ACHIEVE MY GOAL I WILL
ACCOMPLISH THESE TASKS TODAY**

- ☐
- ☐
- ☐
- ☐
- ☐
- ☐
- ☐
- ☐
- ☐
- ☐

- ☐
- ☐
- ☐
- ☐
- ☐
- ☐
- ☐
- ☐
- ☐
- ☐

NOTES

Date: **Day 20**

⊕ TODAYS GOALS TO FOCUS ON

🏗 TO ACHIEVE MY GOAL I WILL
ACCOMPLISH THESE TASKS TODAY

☐ ☐
☐ ☐
☐ ☐
☐ ☐
☐ ☐
☐ ☐
☐ ☐
☐ ☐
☐ ☐
☐ ☐

NOTES

🎯 MY GOALS

⊕ TODAYS GOALS TO FOCUS ON

🪜 TO ACHIEVE MY GOAL I WILL ACCOMPLISH THESE TASKS TODAY

- [ ]
- [ ]
- [ ]
- [ ]
- [ ]
- [ ]
- [ ]
- [ ]
- [ ]
- [ ]

- [ ]
- [ ]
- [ ]
- [ ]
- [ ]
- [ ]
- [ ]
- [ ]
- [ ]
- [ ]

NOTES

Date: # Day 22

🎯 MY GOALS

⊕ TODAYS GOALS TO FOCUS ON

TO ACHIEVE MY GOAL I WILL ACCOMPLISH THESE TASKS TODAY

- [ ]
- [ ]
- [ ]
- [ ]
- [ ]
- [ ]
- [ ]
- [ ]
- [ ]
- [ ]

- [ ]
- [ ]
- [ ]
- [ ]
- [ ]
- [ ]
- [ ]
- [ ]
- [ ]
- [ ]

NOTES

Date:

Day 23

🎯 **MY GOALS**

⊕ **TODAYS GOALS TO FOCUS ON**

🏁 **TO ACHIEVE MY GOAL I WILL ACCOMPLISH THESE TASKS TODAY**

- ☐
- ☐
- ☐
- ☐
- ☐
- ☐
- ☐
- ☐
- ☐
- ☐

- ☐
- ☐
- ☐
- ☐
- ☐
- ☐
- ☐
- ☐
- ☐
- ☐

NOTES

Date: _____ **Day 24**

🎯	MY GOALS

⊕	TODAYS GOALS TO FOCUS ON

🏃	TO ACHIEVE MY GOAL I WILL ACCOMPLISH THESE TASKS TODAY

☐ ☐
☐ ☐
☐ ☐
☐ ☐
☐ ☐
☐ ☐
☐ ☐
☐ ☐
☐ ☐
☐ ☐

NOTES

🎯 MY GOALS

⊕ TODAYS GOALS TO FOCUS ON

🪜 TO ACHIEVE MY GOAL I WILL ACCOMPLISH THESE TASKS TODAY

- [ ]
- [ ]
- [ ]
- [ ]
- [ ]
- [ ]
- [ ]
- [ ]
- [ ]
- [ ]

- [ ]
- [ ]
- [ ]
- [ ]
- [ ]
- [ ]
- [ ]
- [ ]
- [ ]
- [ ]

NOTES

Reflection

"If the plan doesn't work,

change the plan,

not the goal."

Reflection

 AM I ACCOMPLISHING MY GOALS

YES   NO

WHAT HAVE I LEARNT IN THE PAST 25 DAYS?

_____

_____

_____

_____

WHAT NEW IDEAS DO I HAVE?

_____

_____

_____

_____

WHAT NEW SKILLS HAVE I ACQUIRED?

_____

_____

_____

_____

WHAT CHALLENGES I HAD TO OVERCOME?

_____

_____

_____

WHAT ARE MY NEXT STEPS?

_____   _____

_____   _____

Date: _____   # Day 26

🎯	**MY GOALS**

_____

⊕	**TODAYS GOALS TO FOCUS ON**

_____

_____

_____

🏁	**TO ACHIEVE MY GOAL I WILL ACCOMPLISH THESE TASKS TODAY**

_____ ☐   _____ ☐

_____ ☐   _____ ☐

_____ ☐   _____ ☐

_____ ☐   _____ ☐

_____ ☐   _____ ☐

_____ ☐   _____ ☐

_____ ☐   _____ ☐

_____ ☐   _____ ☐

_____ ☐   _____ ☐

_____ ☐   _____ ☐

NOTES

Date: **Day 27**

🎯 **MY GOALS**

⊕ **TODAYS GOALS TO FOCUS ON**

🪜 **TO ACHIEVE MY GOAL I WILL ACCOMPLISH THESE TASKS TODAY**

- [ ]
- [ ]
- [ ]
- [ ]
- [ ]
- [ ]
- [ ]
- [ ]
- [ ]
- [ ]

- [ ]
- [ ]
- [ ]
- [ ]
- [ ]
- [ ]
- [ ]
- [ ]
- [ ]
- [ ]

NOTES

🎯 MY GOALS

◎ TODAYS GOALS TO FOCUS ON

📶 TO ACHIEVE MY GOAL I WILL ACCOMPLISH THESE TASKS TODAY

- ☐
- ☐
- ☐
- ☐
- ☐
- ☐
- ☐
- ☐
- ☐
- ☐

- ☐
- ☐
- ☐
- ☐
- ☐
- ☐
- ☐
- ☐
- ☐

NOTES

Date: **Day 29**

🎯 MY GOALS

⊕ TODAYS GOALS TO FOCUS ON

TO ACHIEVE MY GOAL I WILL ACCOMPLISH THESE TASKS TODAY

- [ ]
- [ ]
- [ ]
- [ ]
- [ ]
- [ ]
- [ ]
- [ ]
- [ ]
- [ ]

- [ ]
- [ ]
- [ ]
- [ ]
- [ ]
- [ ]
- [ ]
- [ ]
- [ ]
- [ ]

NOTES

🎯 MY GOALS

⊕ TODAYS GOALS TO FOCUS ON

🪜 TO ACHIEVE MY GOAL I WILL ACCOMPLISH THESE TASKS TODAY

☐ ☐
☐ ☐
☐ ☐
☐ ☐
☐ ☐
☐ ☐
☐ ☐
☐ ☐
☐ ☐
☐ ☐

NOTES

Date:

Day 31

🎯 MY GOALS

⊕ TODAYS GOALS TO FOCUS ON

TO ACHIEVE MY GOAL I WILL ACCOMPLISH THESE TASKS TODAY

- [ ]
- [ ]
- [ ]
- [ ]
- [ ]
- [ ]
- [ ]
- [ ]
- [ ]
- [ ]

- [ ]
- [ ]
- [ ]
- [ ]
- [ ]
- [ ]
- [ ]
- [ ]
- [ ]
- [ ]

NOTES

🎯 MY GOALS

⊕ TODAYS GOALS TO FOCUS ON

🏁 TO ACHIEVE MY GOAL I WILL ACCOMPLISH THESE TASKS TODAY

- [ ]
- [ ]
- [ ]
- [ ]
- [ ]
- [ ]
- [ ]
- [ ]
- [ ]
- [ ]

NOTES

Date: _____   **Day 33**

⊕ **MY GOALS**

⊕ **TODAYS GOALS TO FOCUS ON**

🪜 **TO ACHIEVE MY GOAL I WILL
ACCOMPLISH THESE TASKS TODAY**

☐   ☐
☐   ☐
☐   ☐
☐   ☐
☐   ☐
☐   ☐
☐   ☐
☐   ☐
☐   ☐
☐   ☐

NOTES

MY GOALS

TODAYS GOALS TO FOCUS ON

TO ACHIEVE MY GOAL I WILL ACCOMPLISH THESE TASKS TODAY

☐   ☐

☐   ☐

☐   ☐

☐   ☐

☐   ☐

☐   ☐

☐   ☐

☐   ☐

☐   ☐

☐   ☐

NOTES

Date: _____ # Day 35

⊕ **TODAYS GOALS TO FOCUS ON**

**TO ACHIEVE MY GOAL I WILL
ACCOMPLISH THESE TASKS TODAY**

☐   ☐

☐   ☐

☐   ☐

☐   ☐

☐   ☐

☐   ☐

☐   ☐

☐   ☐

☐   ☐

☐   ☐

NOTES

Date: _____

Day 36

🎯 MY GOALS

_____

⊕ TODAYS GOALS TO FOCUS ON

_____
_____
_____

▟ TO ACHIEVE MY GOAL I WILL ACCOMPLISH THESE TASKS TODAY

_____ ☐   _____ ☐
_____ ☐   _____ ☐
_____ ☐   _____ ☐
_____ ☐   _____ ☐
_____ ☐   _____ ☐
_____ ☐   _____ ☐
_____ ☐   _____ ☐
_____ ☐   _____ ☐
_____ ☐   _____ ☐
_____ ☐   _____ ☐

NOTES

Date: **Day 37**

🎯 MY GOALS

⊕ TODAYS GOALS TO FOCUS ON

🏁 TO ACHIEVE MY GOAL I WILL ACCOMPLISH THESE TASKS TODAY

- [ ]   [ ]
- [ ]   [ ]
- [ ]   [ ]
- [ ]   [ ]
- [ ]   [ ]
- [ ]   [ ]
- [ ]   [ ]
- [ ]   [ ]
- [ ]   [ ]
- [ ]   [ ]

NOTES

🎯 **MY GOALS**

⊕ **TODAYS GOALS TO FOCUS ON**

🏁 **TO ACHIEVE MY GOAL I WILL ACCOMPLISH THESE TASKS TODAY**

- ☐
- ☐
- ☐
- ☐
- ☐
- ☐
- ☐
- ☐
- ☐
- ☐

- ☐
- ☐
- ☐
- ☐
- ☐
- ☐
- ☐
- ☐
- ☐
- ☐

NOTES

Date: _____ # Day 39

_____

◈ **TODAYS GOALS TO FOCUS ON**

_____
_____
_____

**TO ACHIEVE MY GOAL I WILL
ACCOMPLISH THESE TASKS TODAY**

- [ ] _____ - [ ] _____
- [ ] _____ - [ ] _____
- [ ] _____ - [ ] _____
- [ ] _____ - [ ] _____
- [ ] _____ - [ ] _____
- [ ] _____ - [ ] _____
- [ ] _____ - [ ] _____
- [ ] _____ - [ ] _____
- [ ] _____ - [ ] _____
- [ ] _____ - [ ] _____

NOTES

🎯 MY GOALS

⊕ TODAYS GOALS TO FOCUS ON

▰ TO ACHIEVE MY GOAL I WILL ACCOMPLISH THESE TASKS TODAY

- [ ]
- [ ]
- [ ]
- [ ]
- [ ]
- [ ]
- [ ]
- [ ]
- [ ]
- [ ]

- [ ]
- [ ]
- [ ]
- [ ]
- [ ]
- [ ]
- [ ]
- [ ]
- [ ]
- [ ]

NOTES

Date: _____ # Day 41

⊕ **TODAYS GOALS TO FOCUS ON**

TO ACHIEVE MY GOAL I WILL ACCOMPLISH THESE TASKS TODAY

☐ ☐

☐ ☐

☐ ☐

☐ ☐

☐ ☐

☐ ☐

☐ ☐

☐ ☐

☐ ☐

☐ ☐

NOTES

🎯 MY GOALS

⊕ TODAYS GOALS TO FOCUS ON

🏁 TO ACHIEVE MY GOAL I WILL ACCOMPLISH THESE TASKS TODAY

- [ ]
- [ ]
- [ ]
- [ ]
- [ ]
- [ ]
- [ ]
- [ ]
- [ ]
- [ ]

- [ ]
- [ ]
- [ ]
- [ ]
- [ ]
- [ ]
- [ ]
- [ ]
- [ ]

NOTES

Date: _____

Day 43

🎯 **MY GOALS**

⊕ **TODAYS GOALS TO FOCUS ON**

🏗 **TO ACHIEVE MY GOAL I WILL ACCOMPLISH THESE TASKS TODAY**

- [ ] _____   - [ ] _____
- [ ] _____   - [ ] _____
- [ ] _____   - [ ] _____
- [ ] _____   - [ ] _____
- [ ] _____   - [ ] _____
- [ ] _____   - [ ] _____
- [ ] _____   - [ ] _____
- [ ] _____   - [ ] _____
- [ ] _____   - [ ] _____
- [ ] _____   - [ ] _____

NOTES

🎯 **MY GOALS**

⊕ **TODAYS GOALS TO FOCUS ON**

🏛 **TO ACHIEVE MY GOAL I WILL ACCOMPLISH THESE TASKS TODAY**

☐ ☐
☐ ☐
☐ ☐
☐ ☐
☐ ☐
☐ ☐
☐ ☐
☐ ☐
☐ ☐
☐ ☐

NOTES

Date: _____ # Day 45

🎯	MY GOALS

_____

⊕	TODAYS GOALS TO FOCUS ON

_____
_____
_____

⌐	TO ACHIEVE MY GOAL I WILL ACCOMPLISH THESE TASKS TODAY

_____ ☐   _____ ☐
_____ ☐   _____ ☐
_____ ☐   _____ ☐
_____ ☐   _____ ☐
_____ ☐   _____ ☐
_____ ☐   _____ ☐
_____ ☐   _____ ☐
_____ ☐   _____ ☐
_____ ☐   _____ ☐
_____ ☐   _____ ☐

NOTES

🎯 MY GOALS

⊕ TODAYS GOALS TO FOCUS ON

⫟ TO ACHIEVE MY GOAL I WILL ACCOMPLISH THESE TASKS TODAY

- ☐
- ☐
- ☐
- ☐
- ☐
- ☐
- ☐
- ☐
- ☐
- ☐

- ☐
- ☐
- ☐
- ☐
- ☐
- ☐
- ☐
- ☐
- ☐
- ☐

NOTES

Date: _____   # Day 47

MY GOALS

TODAYS GOALS TO FOCUS ON

**TO ACHIEVE MY GOAL I WILL
ACCOMPLISH THESE TASKS TODAY**

☐	☐
☐	☐
☐	☐
☐	☐
☐	☐
☐	☐
☐	☐
☐	☐
☐	☐
☐	☐

NOTES

Date:

Day 48

🎯 MY GOALS

⊕ TODAYS GOALS TO FOCUS ON

📈 TO ACHIEVE MY GOAL I WILL ACCOMPLISH THESE TASKS TODAY

- [ ]
- [ ]
- [ ]
- [ ]
- [ ]
- [ ]
- [ ]
- [ ]
- [ ]
- [ ]

- [ ]
- [ ]
- [ ]
- [ ]
- [ ]
- [ ]
- [ ]
- [ ]
- [ ]
- [ ]

NOTES

Date: _____ **Day 49**

🎯	MY GOALS

_____

⊕	TODAYS GOALS TO FOCUS ON

_____

_____

_____

🪜	TO ACHIEVE MY GOAL I WILL ACCOMPLISH THESE TASKS TODAY

- ☐
- ☐
- ☐
- ☐
- ☐
- ☐
- ☐
- ☐
- ☐
- ☐

- ☐
- ☐
- ☐
- ☐
- ☐
- ☐
- ☐
- ☐
- ☐
- ☐

NOTES

🎯 **MY GOALS**

⊕ **TODAYS GOALS TO FOCUS ON**

🏁 **TO ACHIEVE MY GOAL I WILL ACCOMPLISH THESE TASKS TODAY**

- ☐   ☐
- ☐   ☐
- ☐   ☐
- ☐   ☐
- ☐   ☐
- ☐   ☐
- ☐   ☐
- ☐   ☐
- ☐   ☐
- ☐   ☐

NOTES

Reflection

"There is no

elevator to success,

you have to take the

stairs."

Reflection

🚩 **AM I ACCOMPLISHING MY GOALS**

           YES   NO

WHAT HAVE I LEARNT IN THE PAST 25 DAYS?

_____

_____

_____

_____

WHAT NEW IDEAS DO I HAVE?

_____

_____

_____

_____

WHAT NEW SKILLS HAVE I ACQUIRED?

_____

_____

_____

_____

WHAT CHALLENGES I HAD TO OVERCOME?

_____

_____

_____

_____

WHAT ARE MY NEXT STEPS?

_____   _____

_____   _____

_____   _____

Day 51

MY GOALS

TODAYS GOALS TO FOCUS ON

TO ACHIEVE MY GOAL I WILL ACCOMPLISH THESE TASKS TODAY

- [ ]   [ ]
- [ ]   [ ]
- [ ]   [ ]
- [ ]   [ ]
- [ ]   [ ]
- [ ]   [ ]
- [ ]   [ ]
- [ ]   [ ]
- [ ]   [ ]
- [ ]   [ ]

NOTES

Date: _____

Day 52

⊙ **MY GOALS**

⊕ **TODAYS GOALS TO FOCUS ON**

TO ACHIEVE MY GOAL I WILL ACCOMPLISH THESE TASKS TODAY

- [ ]
- [ ]
- [ ]
- [ ]
- [ ]
- [ ]
- [ ]
- [ ]
- [ ]
- [ ]

- [ ]
- [ ]
- [ ]
- [ ]
- [ ]
- [ ]
- [ ]
- [ ]
- [ ]
- [ ]

NOTES

🎯 MY GOALS

⊙ TODAYS GOALS TO FOCUS ON

📶 TO ACHIEVE MY GOAL I WILL ACCOMPLISH THESE TASKS TODAY

☐ ☐
☐ ☐
☐ ☐
☐ ☐
☐ ☐
☐ ☐
☐ ☐
☐ ☐
☐ ☐
☐ ☐

NOTES

Date: **Day 54**

🎯 **MY GOALS**

⊕ **TODAYS GOALS TO FOCUS ON**

📶 **TO ACHIEVE MY GOAL I WILL ACCOMPLISH THESE TASKS TODAY**

- [ ]
- [ ]
- [ ]
- [ ]
- [ ]
- [ ]
- [ ]
- [ ]
- [ ]
- [ ]

- [ ]
- [ ]
- [ ]
- [ ]
- [ ]
- [ ]
- [ ]
- [ ]
- [ ]
- [ ]

NOTES

🎯 MY GOALS

⊕ TODAYS GOALS TO FOCUS ON

TO ACHIEVE MY GOAL I WILL ACCOMPLISH THESE TASKS TODAY

- [ ]
- [ ]
- [ ]
- [ ]
- [ ]
- [ ]
- [ ]
- [ ]
- [ ]
- [ ]

- [ ]
- [ ]
- [ ]
- [ ]
- [ ]
- [ ]
- [ ]
- [ ]
- [ ]
- [ ]

NOTES

Date: **Day 56**

🎯 **MY GOALS**

⊕ **TODAYS GOALS TO FOCUS ON**

**TO ACHIEVE MY GOAL I WILL
ACCOMPLISH THESE TASKS TODAY**

☐ ☐
☐ ☐
☐ ☐
☐ ☐
☐ ☐
☐ ☐
☐ ☐
☐ ☐
☐ ☐
☐ ☐

NOTES

🎯 MY GOALS

⊕ TODAYS GOALS TO FOCUS ON

📈 TO ACHIEVE MY GOAL I WILL ACCOMPLISH THESE TASKS TODAY

- [ ]
- [ ]
- [ ]
- [ ]
- [ ]
- [ ]
- [ ]
- [ ]
- [ ]
- [ ]

- [ ]
- [ ]
- [ ]
- [ ]
- [ ]
- [ ]
- [ ]
- [ ]
- [ ]
- [ ]

NOTES

Date: _____

Day 58

⊙	**MY GOALS**

_____

⊕	**TODAYS GOALS TO FOCUS ON**

_____

_____

_____

📶	**TO ACHIEVE MY GOAL I WILL ACCOMPLISH THESE TASKS TODAY**

_____ ☐   _____ ☐

_____ ☐   _____ ☐

_____ ☐   _____ ☐

_____ ☐   _____ ☐

_____ ☐   _____ ☐

_____ ☐   _____ ☐

_____ ☐   _____ ☐

_____ ☐   _____ ☐

_____ ☐   _____ ☐

_____ ☐   _____ ☐

NOTES

🎯 **MY GOALS**

⊕ **TODAYS GOALS TO FOCUS ON**

🏁 **TO ACHIEVE MY GOAL I WILL ACCOMPLISH THESE TASKS TODAY**

☐ ☐
☐ ☐
☐ ☐
☐ ☐
☐ ☐
☐ ☐
☐ ☐
☐ ☐
☐ ☐
☐ ☐

NOTES

Date: _____　　　# Day 60

🎯	MY GOALS

_____

⊙	TODAYS GOALS TO FOCUS ON

_____

_____

_____

📶	TO ACHIEVE MY GOAL I WILL ACCOMPLISH THESE TASKS TODAY

_____ ☐	_____ ☐
_____ ☐	_____ ☐
_____ ☐	_____ ☐
_____ ☐	_____ ☐
_____ ☐	_____ ☐
_____ ☐	_____ ☐
_____ ☐	_____ ☐
_____ ☐	_____ ☐
_____ ☐	_____ ☐
_____ ☐	_____ ☐

NOTES

🎯 MY GOALS

⊕ TODAYS GOALS TO FOCUS ON

🏁 TO ACHIEVE MY GOAL I WILL ACCOMPLISH THESE TASKS TODAY

- [ ]
- [ ]
- [ ]
- [ ]
- [ ]
- [ ]
- [ ]
- [ ]
- [ ]
- [ ]

- [ ]
- [ ]
- [ ]
- [ ]
- [ ]
- [ ]
- [ ]
- [ ]
- [ ]
- [ ]

NOTES

Date: _____   # Day 62

| 🎯 | **MY GOALS** |

| ⊕ | **TODAYS GOALS TO FOCUS ON** |

| 📶 | **TO ACHIEVE MY GOAL I WILL ACCOMPLISH THESE TASKS TODAY** |

- [ ] _____   [ ] _____
- [ ] _____   [ ] _____
- [ ] _____   [ ] _____
- [ ] _____   [ ] _____
- [ ] _____   [ ] _____
- [ ] _____   [ ] _____
- [ ] _____   [ ] _____
- [ ] _____   [ ] _____
- [ ] _____   [ ] _____
- [ ] _____   [ ] _____

| **NOTES** |

Date:

Day 63

🎯	MY GOALS

⊕	TODAYS GOALS TO FOCUS ON

🏁	TO ACHIEVE MY GOAL I WILL ACCOMPLISH THESE TASKS TODAY

- [ ]
- [ ]
- [ ]
- [ ]
- [ ]
- [ ]
- [ ]
- [ ]
- [ ]
- [ ]

NOTES

Day 64

🎯 MY GOALS

⊕ TODAYS GOALS TO FOCUS ON

TO ACHIEVE MY GOAL I WILL ACCOMPLISH THESE TASKS TODAY

	☐		☐
	☐		☐
	☐		☐
	☐		☐
	☐		☐
	☐		☐
	☐		☐
	☐		☐
	☐		☐
	☐		☐

NOTES

🎯 **MY GOALS**

⊕ **TODAYS GOALS TO FOCUS ON**

🏁 **TO ACHIEVE MY GOAL I WILL ACCOMPLISH THESE TASKS TODAY**

	☐		☐
	☐		☐
	☐		☐
	☐		☐
	☐		☐
	☐		☐
	☐		☐
	☐		☐
	☐		☐
	☐		☐

NOTES

Date: _____   **Day 66**

	MY GOALS

	TODAYS GOALS TO FOCUS ON

	TO ACHIEVE MY GOAL I WILL ACCOMPLISH THESE TASKS TODAY

☐   ☐
☐   ☐
☐   ☐
☐   ☐
☐   ☐
☐   ☐
☐   ☐
☐   ☐
☐   ☐
☐

NOTES

Date: _____

Day 67

| 🎯 | **MY GOALS** |

_____

| ⊕ | **TODAYS GOALS TO FOCUS ON** |

_____
_____
_____

| 📶 | **TO ACHIEVE MY GOAL I WILL ACCOMPLISH THESE TASKS TODAY** |

_____ ☐   _____ ☐
_____ ☐   _____ ☐
_____ ☐   _____ ☐
_____ ☐   _____ ☐
_____ ☐   _____ ☐
_____ ☐   _____ ☐
_____ ☐   _____ ☐
_____ ☐   _____ ☐
_____ ☐   _____ ☐
_____ ☐   _____ ☐

| **NOTES** |

Date: **Day 68**

MY GOALS

TODAYS GOALS TO FOCUS ON

TO ACHIEVE MY GOAL I WILL ACCOMPLISH THESE TASKS TODAY

☐ ☐
☐ ☐
☐ ☐
☐ ☐
☐ ☐
☐ ☐
☐ ☐
☐ ☐
☐ ☐
☐ ☐

NOTES

MY GOALS

TODAYS GOALS TO FOCUS ON

TO ACHIEVE MY GOAL I WILL ACCOMPLISH THESE TASKS TODAY

- [ ]
- [ ]
- [ ]
- [ ]
- [ ]
- [ ]
- [ ]
- [ ]
- [ ]
- [ ]

- [ ]
- [ ]
- [ ]
- [ ]
- [ ]
- [ ]
- [ ]
- [ ]
- [ ]
- [ ]

NOTES

Date: _____   # Day 70

🎯 MY GOALS

⊕ TODAYS GOALS TO FOCUS ON

TO ACHIEVE MY GOAL I WILL ACCOMPLISH THESE TASKS TODAY

- ☐
- ☐
- ☐
- ☐
- ☐
- ☐
- ☐
- ☐
- ☐
- ☐

- ☐
- ☐
- ☐
- ☐
- ☐
- ☐
- ☐
- ☐
- ☐
- ☐

NOTES

🎯 MY GOALS

⊕ TODAYS GOALS TO FOCUS ON

🏁 TO ACHIEVE MY GOAL I WILL ACCOMPLISH THESE TASKS TODAY

- [ ]   [ ]
- [ ]   [ ]
- [ ]   [ ]
- [ ]   [ ]
- [ ]   [ ]
- [ ]   [ ]
- [ ]   [ ]
- [ ]   [ ]
- [ ]   [ ]
- [ ]   [ ]

NOTES

Day 72

🎯 MY GOALS

⊕ TODAYS GOALS TO FOCUS ON

🪜 TO ACHIEVE MY GOAL I WILL ACCOMPLISH THESE TASKS TODAY

- ☐
- ☐
- ☐
- ☐
- ☐
- ☐
- ☐
- ☐
- ☐
- ☐

- ☐
- ☐
- ☐
- ☐
- ☐
- ☐
- ☐
- ☐
- ☐
- ☐

NOTES

Date:

Day 73

🎯 **MY GOALS**

⊕ **TODAYS GOALS TO FOCUS ON**

🪜 **TO ACHIEVE MY GOAL I WILL ACCOMPLISH THESE TASKS TODAY**

☐   ☐

☐   ☐

☐   ☐

☐   ☐

☐   ☐

☐   ☐

☐   ☐

☐   ☐

☐   ☐

☐   ☐

NOTES

Date: **Day 74**

🎯 **MY GOALS**

⊕ **TODAYS GOALS TO FOCUS ON**

🏃 **TO ACHIEVE MY GOAL I WILL ACCOMPLISH THESE TASKS TODAY**

- [ ]
- [ ]
- [ ]
- [ ]
- [ ]
- [ ]
- [ ]
- [ ]
- [ ]
- [ ]

NOTES

MY GOALS

TODAYS GOALS TO FOCUS ON

TO ACHIEVE MY GOAL I WILL ACCOMPLISH THESE TASKS TODAY

- [ ]   [ ]
- [ ]   [ ]
- [ ]   [ ]
- [ ]   [ ]
- [ ]   [ ]
- [ ]   [ ]
- [ ]   [ ]
- [ ]   [ ]
- [ ]   [ ]
- [ ]   [ ]

NOTES

DAY 75

Reflection

"When the 'why' is clear,

the 'how' is easy."

Reflection

AM I ACCOMPLISHING MY GOALS

YES   NO

WHAT HAVE I LEARNT IN THE PAST 25 DAYS?

_____

_____

_____

_____

_____

WHAT NEW IDEAS DO I HAVE?

_____

_____

_____

_____

_____

WHAT NEW SKILLS HAVE I ACQUIRED?

_____

_____

_____

_____

_____

WHAT CHALLENGES I HAD TO OVERCOME?

_____

_____

_____

_____

WHAT ARE MY NEXT STEPS?

_____   _____

_____   _____

🎯 MY GOALS

⊙ TODAYS GOALS TO FOCUS ON

TO ACHIEVE MY GOAL I WILL ACCOMPLISH THESE TASKS TODAY

- [ ]
- [ ]
- [ ]
- [ ]
- [ ]
- [ ]
- [ ]
- [ ]
- [ ]
- [ ]

- [ ]
- [ ]
- [ ]
- [ ]
- [ ]
- [ ]
- [ ]
- [ ]
- [ ]
- [ ]

NOTES

Date: **Day 77**

MY GOALS

TODAYS GOALS TO FOCUS ON

TO ACHIEVE MY GOAL I WILL ACCOMPLISH THESE TASKS TODAY

- ☐
- ☐
- ☐
- ☐
- ☐
- ☐
- ☐
- ☐
- ☐
- ☐

- ☐
- ☐
- ☐
- ☐
- ☐
- ☐
- ☐
- ☐
- ☐
- ☐

NOTES

Date: _____   # Day 78

🎯 MY GOALS

⊕ TODAYS GOALS TO FOCUS ON

🪜 TO ACHIEVE MY GOAL I WILL ACCOMPLISH THESE TASKS TODAY

	☐		☐
	☐		☐
	☐		☐
	☐		☐
	☐		☐
	☐		☐
	☐		☐
	☐		☐
	☐		☐
	☐		☐

NOTES

Date: **Day 79**

MY GOALS

TODAYS GOALS TO FOCUS ON

TO ACHIEVE MY GOAL I WILL ACCOMPLISH THESE TASKS TODAY

- [ ]
- [ ]
- [ ]
- [ ]
- [ ]
- [ ]
- [ ]
- [ ]
- [ ]
- [ ]

- [ ]
- [ ]
- [ ]
- [ ]
- [ ]
- [ ]
- [ ]
- [ ]
- [ ]
- [ ]

NOTES

MY GOALS

TODAYS GOALS TO FOCUS ON

TO ACHIEVE MY GOAL I WILL ACCOMPLISH THESE TASKS TODAY

- [ ]
- [ ]
- [ ]
- [ ]
- [ ]
- [ ]
- [ ]
- [ ]
- [ ]
- [ ]

- [ ]
- [ ]
- [ ]
- [ ]
- [ ]
- [ ]
- [ ]
- [ ]
- [ ]
- [ ]

NOTES

Date: **Day 81**

🎯 **MY GOALS**

⊕ **TODAYS GOALS TO FOCUS ON**

🏁 **TO ACHIEVE MY GOAL I WILL ACCOMPLISH THESE TASKS TODAY**

☐ ☐
☐ ☐
☐ ☐
☐ ☐
☐ ☐
☐ ☐
☐ ☐
☐ ☐
☐ ☐
☐ ☐

NOTES

Date: _____

Day 82

🎯 MY GOALS

⊕ TODAYS GOALS TO FOCUS ON

🏁 TO ACHIEVE MY GOAL I WILL ACCOMPLISH THESE TASKS TODAY

	☐		☐
	☐		☐
	☐		☐
	☐		☐
	☐		☐
	☐		☐
	☐		☐
	☐		☐
	☐		☐
	☐		☐

NOTES

Day 83

MY GOALS

TODAYS GOALS TO FOCUS ON

TO ACHIEVE MY GOAL I WILL ACCOMPLISH THESE TASKS TODAY

- [ ]
- [ ]
- [ ]
- [ ]
- [ ]
- [ ]
- [ ]
- [ ]
- [ ]
- [ ]

- [ ]
- [ ]
- [ ]
- [ ]
- [ ]
- [ ]
- [ ]
- [ ]
- [ ]

NOTES

MY GOALS

TODAYS GOALS TO FOCUS ON

TO ACHIEVE MY GOAL I WILL ACCOMPLISH THESE TASKS TODAY

- [ ]
- [ ]
- [ ]
- [ ]
- [ ]
- [ ]
- [ ]
- [ ]
- [ ]
- [ ]

- [ ]
- [ ]
- [ ]
- [ ]
- [ ]
- [ ]
- [ ]
- [ ]
- [ ]
- [ ]

NOTES

Date: _____   # Day 85

🎯	MY GOALS

⊕	TODAYS GOALS TO FOCUS ON

📶	TO ACHIEVE MY GOAL I WILL ACCOMPLISH THESE TASKS TODAY

- [ ]
- [ ]
- [ ]
- [ ]
- [ ]
- [ ]
- [ ]
- [ ]
- [ ]
- [ ]

- [ ]
- [ ]
- [ ]
- [ ]
- [ ]
- [ ]
- [ ]
- [ ]
- [ ]
- [ ]

NOTES

Date: _____ **Day 86**

🎯 **MY GOALS**

⊕ **TODAYS GOALS TO FOCUS ON**

🏁 **TO ACHIEVE MY GOAL I WILL ACCOMPLISH THESE TASKS TODAY**

- [ ] _____   [ ] _____
- [ ] _____   [ ] _____
- [ ] _____   [ ] _____
- [ ] _____   [ ] _____
- [ ] _____   [ ] _____
- [ ] _____   [ ] _____
- [ ] _____   [ ] _____
- [ ] _____   [ ] _____
- [ ] _____   [ ] _____
- [ ] _____   [ ] _____

NOTES

🎯 **MY GOALS**

⊙ **TODAYS GOALS TO FOCUS ON**

🏃 **TO ACHIEVE MY GOAL I WILL ACCOMPLISH THESE TASKS TODAY**

- ☐
- ☐
- ☐
- ☐
- ☐
- ☐
- ☐
- ☐
- ☐
- ☐

- ☐
- ☐
- ☐
- ☐
- ☐
- ☐
- ☐
- ☐
- ☐
- ☐

NOTES

🎯 MY GOALS

⊕ TODAYS GOALS TO FOCUS ON

🪜 TO ACHIEVE MY GOAL I WILL ACCOMPLISH THESE TASKS TODAY

- [ ]
- [ ]
- [ ]
- [ ]
- [ ]
- [ ]
- [ ]
- [ ]
- [ ]
- [ ]

- [ ]
- [ ]
- [ ]
- [ ]
- [ ]
- [ ]
- [ ]
- [ ]
- [ ]
- [ ]

NOTES

Date: _____

Day 89

🎯 MY GOALS

_____

⊕ TODAYS GOALS TO FOCUS ON

_____
_____
_____

📶 TO ACHIEVE MY GOAL I WILL ACCOMPLISH THESE TASKS TODAY

- ☐ _____ ☐ _____
- ☐ _____ ☐ _____
- ☐ _____ ☐ _____
- ☐ _____ ☐ _____
- ☐ _____ ☐ _____
- ☐ _____ ☐ _____
- ☐ _____ ☐ _____
- ☐ _____ ☐ _____
- ☐ _____ ☐ _____
- ☐ _____ ☐ _____

NOTES

MY GOALS

TODAYS GOALS TO FOCUS ON

TO ACHIEVE MY GOAL I WILL ACCOMPLISH THESE TASKS TODAY

- [ ]
- [ ]
- [ ]
- [ ]
- [ ]
- [ ]
- [ ]
- [ ]
- [ ]
- [ ]

- [ ]
- [ ]
- [ ]
- [ ]
- [ ]
- [ ]
- [ ]
- [ ]
- [ ]
- [ ]

NOTES

Date: _____ # Day 91

🎯 MY GOALS

_____

⊕ TODAYS GOALS TO FOCUS ON

_____
_____
_____

📶 TO ACHIEVE MY GOAL I WILL ACCOMPLISH THESE TASKS TODAY

_____	☐	_____	☐
_____	☐	_____	☐
_____	☐	_____	☐
_____	☐	_____	☐
_____	☐	_____	☐
_____	☐	_____	☐
_____	☐	_____	☐
_____	☐	_____	☐
_____	☐	_____	☐
_____	☐	_____	☐

NOTES

🎯 MY GOALS

⊕ TODAYS GOALS TO FOCUS ON

⚑ TO ACHIEVE MY GOAL I WILL ACCOMPLISH THESE TASKS TODAY

- ☐
- ☐
- ☐
- ☐
- ☐
- ☐
- ☐
- ☐
- ☐
- ☐

- ☐
- ☐
- ☐
- ☐
- ☐
- ☐
- ☐
- ☐
- ☐
- ☐

NOTES

🎯 MY GOALS

⊕ TODAYS GOALS TO FOCUS ON

📈 TO ACHIEVE MY GOAL I WILL ACCOMPLISH THESE TASKS TODAY

- [ ]
- [ ]
- [ ]
- [ ]
- [ ]
- [ ]
- [ ]
- [ ]
- [ ]
- [ ]
- [ ]
- [ ]
- [ ]
- [ ]
- [ ]
- [ ]
- [ ]
- [ ]
- [ ]
- [ ]

NOTES

Date: **Day 94**

MY GOALS

TODAYS GOALS TO FOCUS ON

TO ACHIEVE MY GOAL I WILL
ACCOMPLISH THESE TASKS TODAY

☐   ☐
☐   ☐
☐   ☐
☐   ☐
☐   ☐
☐   ☐
☐   ☐
☐   ☐
☐   ☐
☐

NOTES

Date: **Day 95**

MY GOALS

TODAYS GOALS TO FOCUS ON

**TO ACHIEVE MY GOAL I WILL
ACCOMPLISH THESE TASKS TODAY**

NOTES

Date:

Day 96

🎯 MY GOALS

⊕ TODAYS GOALS TO FOCUS ON

⌐ TO ACHIEVE MY GOAL I WILL ACCOMPLISH THESE TASKS TODAY

- [ ]
- [ ]
- [ ]
- [ ]
- [ ]
- [ ]
- [ ]
- [ ]
- [ ]
- [ ]

- [ ]
- [ ]
- [ ]
- [ ]
- [ ]
- [ ]
- [ ]
- [ ]
- [ ]
- [ ]

NOTES

Date: _____ ## Day 97

🎯	MY GOALS

_____

⊕	TODAYS GOALS TO FOCUS ON

_____
_____
_____

🏁	TO ACHIEVE MY GOAL I WILL ACCOMPLISH THESE TASKS TODAY

- ☐ _____ ☐ _____
- ☐ _____ ☐ _____
- ☐ _____ ☐ _____
- ☐ _____ ☐ _____
- ☐ _____ ☐ _____
- ☐ _____ ☐ _____
- ☐ _____ ☐ _____
- ☐ _____ ☐ _____
- ☐ _____ ☐ _____
- ☐ _____ ☐ _____

NOTES

Day 98

🎯 MY GOALS

⊕ TODAYS GOALS TO FOCUS ON

TO ACHIEVE MY GOAL I WILL ACCOMPLISH THESE TASKS TODAY

- ☐
- ☐
- ☐
- ☐
- ☐
- ☐
- ☐
- ☐
- ☐
- ☐

- ☐
- ☐
- ☐
- ☐
- ☐
- ☐
- ☐
- ☐
- ☐
- ☐

NOTES

Day 99

MY GOALS

TODAYS GOALS TO FOCUS ON

TO ACHIEVE MY GOAL I WILL ACCOMPLISH THESE TASKS TODAY

- [ ]
- [ ]
- [ ]
- [ ]
- [ ]
- [ ]
- [ ]
- [ ]
- [ ]
- [ ]

- [ ]
- [ ]
- [ ]
- [ ]
- [ ]
- [ ]
- [ ]
- [ ]

NOTES

Date: _____   # Day 100

🎯 **MY GOALS**

⊙ **TODAYS GOALS TO FOCUS ON**

📶 **TO ACHIEVE MY GOAL I WILL ACCOMPLISH THESE TASKS TODAY**

- ☐   ☐
- ☐   ☐
- ☐   ☐
- ☐   ☐
- ☐   ☐
- ☐   ☐
- ☐   ☐
- ☐   ☐
- ☐   ☐
- ☐   ☐

NOTES

Reflection

"You are never too old to set

another goal or dream a new

dream".

Reflection

CONGRATULATIONS YOU MADE IT TO 100 DAYS. WERE
YOU SUCCESSFUL IN REACHING YOUR GOALS?

YES   NO

WHAT HAVE I LEARNED IN THE PAST 100 OF
GOAL PLANNING DAYS?

_____
_____
_____
_____
_____

WHAT NEW IDEAS DO I HAVE?

_____
_____
_____
_____

WHAT NEW SKILLS HAVE I ACQUIRED?

_____
_____
_____
_____

WHAT CHALLENGES I HAD TO OVERCOME?

_____
_____
_____

WHAT ARE MY NEXT STEPS?

_____   _____
_____   _____

Notes

Notes

Notes

Notes

Notes

Notes

Notes

Notes

Notes

Notes

Notes

Notes

Made in the USA
Las Vegas, NV
03 January 2025

15712844R00079